The Sleep Road

Stewart Sanderson

Poems in *The Sleep Road* have previously appeared in:
Anthropocene, The Dark Horse, Dark Mountain, Edwin Morgan
Poetry Award 2020: Poems by the Shortlisted Poets, Gutter,
Иностранная литература, Lyrical Aye Poems, Modern Poetry in
Translation, Northwords Now, Places (artist book with Rosalind
Sanderson), PN Review, Poetry Birmingham Literary Journal,
Poetry Wales, Stand.

* * *

Published in 2021 by Tapsalteerie
9 Anderson Terrace, Tarland
Aberdeenshire, AB34 4YH
www.tapsalteerie.co.uk

Cover Image: 'Juniperus communis L', collected in the
Cairngorms by John Ball, 1839. Courtsey of the Smithsonian
Institute (Creative Commons Licence).

ISBN: 978-1-9162148-5-9

Printed and bound by Imprint Digital, Upton Pyne, Devon.

For Karen

Contents

Unland

I know a word
  for the weather-beaten places

    a word for where nothing
    will grow but what
  we cannot eat

    for where the land
      is worn at and washed

    away by waters
  which erode
      soil as the stillness

      does this word for where
  no nation matters

      for where the little
  lochans lap
    up ever so lightly

    at the louring sky
  and hidden

    drove roads wind
    downhill towards
infinity

Gorselight

yellow lamps
in a night of thorns

the petals flicker
the bush burns

The Thistle Bird

I make this poem as softly as I can
for fear of frightening the only word
I need, which landing in Estonian
becomes *ohakalind*, the thistle bird:
a skittish shyness, shifting in a blurred
flitter of feathers, through the dappled trees
around Viljandi, where the silence, stirred
up by its tiny wingbeats and a breeze
blown off the Urals, weighs the centuries
through which that word, *ohakalind*, has passed –
weighs up the alternate realities
in which little *Eesti* failed to last.

Goldfinch. *Ohakalind*. Another name
for it is *lasair-choille*, forest flame.

Dunadd

A hollow like a human foot
incised into the living rock
which I filled with my walking boot
one day, daring the sky to crack

at my temerity: but no
somehow the vault of heaven held
and holds, however many go
to do what only one, who ruled

the rest, was ever meant to do –
to stand where he might see his lands
unfold, then swear he would stay true
to what he saw. The image sends

a little tremor down my spine:
it would be good to promise this;
to feel, behind you in a line
the others who came to this place

before you did, to prove their worth
by slipping off their hidebound shoes
and, bootless, promising the earth –
its browns, its greens, its greys and blues.

Pictish

Listen to the wind
where this language was –
the whisper as it passes
through the long
grass at St. Vigeans,
the leaves at Aberlemno.

Read on past the pause
where its king list
ebbs away into the waters
of a new tongue: so the river
Ewe runs downhill
towards its sea loch.

Reach out and touch
the topsoil to which
its syllables remain
attached: an anchor
lodged in sand years after
the ship has rotted.

Throw one last log
on the fire as you pronounce
their names – *Nechtan* and *Brude*,
Drostan and *Drest* – then let
them blend like smoke does
with the midnight air.

The Wind's Poem

On Peniel Heugh I abandoned a poem
leaving it there for the wind to finish

however it would – writing its story
in the emptiness where my words ended

and its world began: a line break yawning
as a crag does, over depths in silence –

strata where the weather thickens
like black earth; the air forever searching

for the same unspoken syllable
soil seeks, that broken consonant

it longs to speak, without a vowel
to soothe it into sound, to sain

speech into it, struck dumb between
the Scottish Borders and the Urals.

A Lump of Quartz

I found the goodness of this world
exposed out on the high moraine
of Ben Dorain: a lump of quartz
worn smooth by centuries of rain.

No larger than a small child's fist
I felt its cold weight fill my palm:
a heavy lightness, like the sweep
of some old Hebridean psalm.

I turned it: marbled white and grey
now dull, now dazzling as it shone –
it could have been a fold of fat
cut from an ice-bound mastodon.

Or, dropped there by a glacier,
the still heart of a fossil bird –
grandsire to archaeopteryx
for which science has, as yet, no word.

A pebble to put in your mouth
and roll till you had learned to speak –
a simple thing to throw away
after an hour, a day, a week.

A single stone containing all
compassion, virtue, tenderness –
waxing and waning with the ebb
and flood tide of our tendencies.

Tynsale

'The losing (*of* possessions, etc.); loss, destruction, harm, detriment.' – *Dictionary of the Scots Language*

A term for when the tin's been sold
and all the tinsel taken down –
for when we feel a tingling cold

or find a shot stag's hollow crown
out on the moor, then count the tines
to tell how many years have blown

past while it wandered in the pines
and windy places, where our lack
takes solid form: a wall which dwines

by increments into the slack
ground by a freshly-planted wood
of firs, spread like a dark-green crack

through fields where people's houses stood.
Tynsale: a word we're losing now
as language thins; a word which could

come back, perhaps, teaching us how
to talk about what's happening
and as we walk into the lowe

of our own *tynsale*, find something
to sing about, be it so small
as this one word, which we let ring

despite the bleakness of it all.

The Lichens of Scotland (1)

Lettered Lichen | Map Lichen
Black-green Lichen | Wrinkled Lichen

Porous warty Lichen | Black nobbed Lichen
Black-nobb'd Dyer's Lichen | Black nobb'd fuscous Lichen

Black and white mix'd Lichen | Bluish Lichen, with black warts
Vernal Lichen | Pale Rock Lichen

Red-spangled tartareous Lichen | Mealy Beech Lichen
Grey orbicular Lichen | Coralline Lichen

Flesh-colour'd Mushroom Lichen | Brown Mushroom Lichen
Orange Lichen | Yellow farinaceous or crusted Lichen

Large yellow-saucer'd Dyer's Lichen | Pale glaucous Lichen
Brownish Lichen | Black cupped Lichen

Crawfish-eye Lichen | Greenish chestnut-shielded Lichen
Cartilaginous Lichen | Grey-blue pitted Lichen

Ogham

I

The Brandsbutt Stone

It must
resist the philologist
almost unsuccessfully
then as it seems to yield
allow a little
doubt to
drift like woodsmoke
or coastal haar
across the characters, ever
redeemed and ever
negated by their many
silences.

II

The Buckquoy Spindle-Whorl

Before it is misunderstood
each weathered carving
names nothing; is
deprived of speech, though
as a poem occasionally
can, still manages
to communicate something
albeit only our
need to express ourselves
in whichever
material is nearest
lest we be forgotten.

III

The Lunnasting Stone

Even
the lichen
tricks us as it
etches away and so
confounds
us till all
hope has been
erased of our
translating half
these stories lost in
stone.

And again
how the wind
has worn
them till only
the faintest trace stays
anchored
nearly yet
not quite reduced to
nothingness.

How the rain
conspires against
consonant and
vowel as it
veers in
everlastingly
voluminous and
vulture-like.

No words can
express
how much
has vanished
though nonetheless I
offer these words
now to sweeten
sorrow.

Sleepwalking

the harper's sleep | the road to insanity
the propaganda of truth | the multitude of dreams

the smoke of heather | the silent consent
the state and the parties | the white hound and the deer

the flee on the gridiron | the activity of the mob
the pride in necessity | the direction of the wind

the wind that brings strangers | the criminals in the leadership
the lowest thief and murderer | the gelding breaking wind

the wind of frost | the essence of political action
the barbed wire | the rest is sleep and dozing

the sleep of dogs | the road to total domination
the equality of all citizens | the precipitous red rocks

the white horse at the mill-door | the imminent collapse
the end of human history | the sheep's sleep in the briars

Highland Vowels

A

the black rain at the springing of roots | the black desolate moor
the black-mouthed MacDiarmids | the black spikes of small oats

E

the white lame gelding | the white-faced yellow calf
white bargains when the snow comes | the white sword of light

I

the song of the red one | the red weed from the dunghill
the red man scornful | the red coat a coward

U

the worst of fuel, an alder green | a green winter | a green Yule
green is the grass of the least-trodden field | green are the hills
    we are far from

O

the crow likes her greedy blue chick | the big blue-eyed
    man from Moy
blue are the hills we are far from | the mountain blue in
    the distance

Cowlairs

Passing Cowlairs on the Glasgow train
one grey morning, I felt the engine slow
and glancing through a thin, translucent pane
of glasslike stuff, saw tower blocks and below
them waste ground – bracken wet from last night's rain
and scrabbly brambles, managing to grow
in the embankment by the railway line:
their presence struck me as a hopeful sign.

The train stood still, without a platform near
for maybe half a minute, who knows why –
the reason for our stop was no more clear
than was the bleary West of Scotland sky –
but as we waited there I saw a deer,
a young red doe, retreating with a shy
sense of occasion through the dripping ferns:
one of those sights on which existence turns

for half a second. Then the deer was gone –
lost in the undergrowth beside the track –
and suddenly the train was moving on
to Queen Street Station through a tunnel's black
integument, then out into the sun.
All day it followed me around: the lack
of what had made the whole world rich and strange
while somewhere up ahead the signals changed.

Seeking

That red kite I saw two days ago
from the cottage window
feeling its way over a furrow
in the wind: I know
what it sought in the ebb and flow
of air, in every undertow
and updraft – ready to throw
the rough pasture below
where a mouse might burrow
towards its talons. Let me show
you something else: a cloud's slow
progress, swaddling the snow
capped Cairngorms, which grow
as the rain falls back. Rimbaud
would have found both E and O
in such a prospect – the stark glow
of the peaks, wrapped in their indigo
grey shawls – and A in a crow
as it swithers to and fro
before setting down, with no
less grace than a noh
artiste, on a fencepost. So
the hand, finding a radio
station, lets the dial go.

Hill Fort

A palimpsest of people's lives
this hilltop is a manuscript
sections of which have not survived:
see, where the earthen banks have slipped.

Then there are lacunae where
the ploughman – not unlike a scribe
reusing rolls – has brought his share
through old work, tossing stones aside.

A fragment, half of which has gone
to feed the wind – insatiable
and writing its own story on
the weathered vellum of the hill.

Even the pollen, buried deep
below my feet, has tales to tell –
still dreaming, in its wintry sleep
of when the ice sheets rose and fell.

A reading knowledge of the land
reveals what is recorded here
and though it's hard to understand
the underlying sense is clear.

As evening falls, I walk across
this written and unwritten ground –
my footprints footnotes to its loss:
a poem waiting to be found.

An Unstatistical Account

the names of the hills
the soil upon the hills

the foot of the hills
the benty hills

the pasture hills
the surrounding hills

the hills of Scotia
the hills lying south

*

down to the sea
to the open sea

the hill to the sea
the town, next the sea

an arm of the sea
communication with the sea

the retreat of the sea
from sea to sea

*

a small island
the whole island

the Mainland, or principal island
the small flat rocky island

parts of this island
this part of the island

division of the island
extending across the island

*

the grove of oak trees
any grove of oak trees

trees about farm towns
geen and garden trees

trees of various kinds
one hundred ash trees

the trees, by being left
the trees thereafter

*

moss begins
a few spots of moss

portions of moss
a given quantity of moss

the moss in question
the whole body of moss

the deepest moss
the softness of the moss

*

small farms
the smallest farms

lost in the large farms
the farms being fitted for sheep

an evil attending large farms
the lands in great farms

improved farms
the farms have not been measured

*

this people
they are like other people

poor people
frugal and laborious people

common people
the very lowest of the people

people in general
our own people

*

we consider the climate
the climate is good

the climate is healthy
the climate is cold

the climate of Bendothy
the climate in this parish

the climate of the place
adapted to the climate

*

a thousand hills
overflowed by the sea

then in the island
trees lying in all directions

the total abolition of the moss
the monopoly of farms

the passing of people
the climate is so unsteady

The Sleep Road

over the moor
we walk together

down the road
Wade's redcoats made

langsyne perhaps –
or just our steps

sifted like sleet
night after night

a metaphor
for where we are

wearing a line
in each day's mountain

a goat track cut
in wakeful granite

the winding path
of our shared breath

The Lichens of Scotland (II)

Dark purple Dyer's Lichen | Small black Cork, or Lichen
Olive Lichen | Curled Jelly Lichen

Crested Jelly Lichen | Common yellow Wall-Lichen
Inflated Lichen | Starry Lichen

Small-cut brown Lichen | Lead-colour'd spongy Lichen
Crowned Lichen, or Burgess's Lichen

Hairy or ciliated Lichen | Eatable Iceland Lichen
Lungwort Lichen | Grey-horned branny Lichen

Narrow-cut warty Lichen | Beaked Lichen
Great long-leaf'd wrinkled Lichen | Common ragged
    hoary Lichen

Common yellow Tree Lichen | Sulphur-green Rose Lichen
Smooth endive-leav'd Lichen | Common blue
    curled Lichen

Bat's-wing Lichen | Little palmated cluster Lichen
Tender membranaceous Lichen | Livid brown Lichen,
    with reversed shields

Gaeltacht

Stacked peats on Cnoc a' Chridhe
in the early morning twilight.

The hound's tongue licking
at the fox's severed paw.

The Red Panda

Don't tell me yet how few there are
still living in our wounded world
circling a slowly dying star.

For now let me become one, curled
upon a pine branch, sound asleep
despite the cold wind, which has birled

all day about the forest, deep
and filled with snow, falling to hide
my tracks. The mountains here are steep.

The wild, uncharted woods are wide
enough for me: a million trees
and into winter they elide.

Let me drowse on a little, please
as dreamed clouds thicken and below
imaginary rivers freeze.

Let me let go of what I know
is happening, just for a while
and then I promise you can show

me all you have to; promise I'll
see through this softly swirling white
and not meet darkness with denial.

For now let early evening light
fade through my red fur: this comes first
though soon, as Himalayan night

sets in, I swear to face the worst.

The Solan

Goose
or gannet, 'whose
     smell is so powerful that he is'
     under no circumstances
          'cooked within doors', is the largest

sea-
bird of any
     to be found in the North Atlantic
     combing the oceanic
          distance in search of sustenance

or
perched by the score
     on perilous ledges high above
     the waves as they surge and shove
          at the foundations of the land.

Scott,
a writer not
     to be deterred by powerful smells
     insofar as his novels
          required, describes the 'relishing'

taste –
fish interlaced
     with pheasant – of a well-smoked solan
     which till recently formed an
          important part of our cuisine.

In
Boece's Latin
    Chronicle, or else the translation
    into Scots made by one John
        Bellenden, we read how the Bass

Rock –
that trachyte block
    three hundred million years or so
    in age, covered with guano –
        bears 'an incredible noumer

of'
(hard not to love
    his spelling) 'soland geis; nocht unlik
    to thir fowlis' (with a stick
        I could eat such words) which Pliny

calls
'see ernis': squalls
    of them rising and falling round their
    black fastness; filling the air
        with the dissonance of their song.

The Call of the Lapwing

Thevisnek, thevisnek –
the creak of a rope.

A verse I recite
to save us all from swinging.

To Artio

Because my love is like a bronze bear shambling
through thorn bushes towards a Gallo-Roman
lady, I, Licinia Sabinilla,
address this poem

to both your bodies, Artio – the woman
balancing a basketful of apples
between her knees, but also that wild creature
snuffling and whiffling

over gorse and sweetbriar, beseeching her second
self with doleful, less than human eyes to let
her taste even the worst-bruised windfalls, stolen
from some man's orchard.

Bone

,

         s

.   A petition

,   a prayer

.   *Douglas*

.   O

.   E

.

         id

.

   Isl

.

    baen

,

    precatio

,   oratio

;   *boon*

,   petitio

,   gratis
                    acceptio

,   mendicatio

,   G
.   Andr
.   A
.   S
                    ben

,   *bene*

,   id.

Breath

,

s.   1. Opinion ;

sentiments ;
tendency of thought ;

'I wad fain hear his *breath* about this business.'

As A. S. *braeth* ,
signifies
spiritus ,

the E. word is here used like Fr. *esprit* ,

for mind ,
thought ,
opinion ,
disposition ,
inclination ,

2. *In a breath* ;

in a moment ,
S.

The Lichens of Scotland (III)

Little dark-vein'd Lichen | Ash-colour'd ground
 Liverwort, or Lichen
Villous-wood Lichen | Brown flat-shielded Lichen

Pitted warty Lichen, with broad glaucous leaves |
 Lovely-green Lichen, with reddish shields
Pale blue scallop'd Lichen, bearing dark green balls |
 Socket Lichen

Saffron Lichen, with flat shields | Grey cloudy Lichen,
 tawny underneath
Complicated cloudy Lichen | Singed or blistered Lichen

Frizled Hair-button Lichen | Black-grey Lichen, with
 little black warts
Sad colour'd crumpled Lichen, with black curled warts |
 Little smooth dusky rock Lichen

Dusky rock Lichen, black and fibrous underneath |
 Scarlet-tipp'd Cup Lichen
Radiated Lichen | Common Cup-Moss, or Lichen

Serrated Cup Lichen | Little Trumpet Lichen
Elk's Horn Lichen | Tall slender Lichen

Branched Lichen, with scarlet heads | Branched
 Cornucopia Lichen
Horned or Skewer Lichen | Clumsey Lichen, with
 subulate stalks and dented cups

Inchkeith

One of the iron-tongued annalists records
how James the Fourth, who knew nine languages,
grew captivated by the silences
in which the secret origin of words
lies hidden from us. Listening to the birds
whose speech comes closer to the deity's
than ours, he asked the wind what language is,
obsessed with glottal stops and voiceless surds.

At length two low-born infants – seized or bought,
the writer doesn't specify – were sent
off to Inchkeith, an island in the Forth.
Raised by a deaf and dumb wet nurse, it's thought
they learned some Hebrew from the immanent
while showers of hail descended from the north.

A Renouncing

'Item, gevin at the kingis command iij Septembris, to John
Broun, lutare, at his passage our sey to leve his craft, v.li.'
 – *Lord High Treasurer of Scotland's Accounts, 1474*

One by one, he snapped the strings
bringing a borrowed kitchen knife
    fifteen times down
upon an instrument which kings
once wept to hear, whose subtle strife
    he had outgrown.

Or grown tired of – and though it stung
to listen to each twangling sound
    the tautened gut
made as he freed it from its long
rigidity, somehow he found
    the strength to cut.

The strength to break, over one knee
that neck on which his left hand danced
    in Linlithgow
and Edinburgh, while royalty
took surfeit of love's food, entranced
    with een aglow.

The bitter will to put his right
straight through the body like a tear-
    drop of soft wood
then give all to the fire as night
set in, a dark sail riding near
    upon the flood.

Those Unheard

Skene Mandore MS, ca. 1620

I

The Flowres of the Forrest

Grief, get away –
be yourself elsewhere.

Don't bide here
gathering like rainclouds.

Now gladness hides
beyond dark elms.

Dust whispers
and grows greedy.

Yesterday evening
their shadows met us.

Dusk brings voices
until echoes die.

Returning singly
girls stand round waiting.

Anemones utter
aicill underfoot.

II

*Thou Wilt Then Goe
and Leave Me Her*

Rivers deepen
dividing lands.

Musk lingers –
rises, dampens.

Yellow roses
rotting slowly.

Music somewhere
dwines, diminished.

Roads lengthen
through grey glens.

Through mountains
slumbering.

Though I'm quiet
you listen.

This silence –
your sense drifting.

III

*I Will Not Goe to My
Bed till I Suld Die*

Drinking despite
the heavy day tomorrow.

Again despite
these sorrows, drinking whisky.

Drinking despite
the hour, dead midnight.

Barleycorn visions –
whisky dreams.

While darkness beckons
howffs bring abundance.

Muscat and malmsey
electrify dreich winters.

Drams delight –
dancers birl on floorboards.

Soon drinking
will disappear.

The Wealth of Nations

It's night, millennia ago
and in the Beaker People's tongue
a man or woman (we don't know)
is turning silence into song.

Tuning the words, he or she tests
their torque, presses at prosody
until at length the whole work rests
in an achieved economy.

This way wealth is created out
of any raw material
even anxiety and doubt –
that bit of us which won't stay still

or be content just listening
to countless questions we can't find
an answer to; which needs something
to whisper at the howling wind.

Held in the mind and handed on
from one lifetime down to the next
the Beaker poet's poem is gone –
a few cracked pots its only text.

And isn't this a fair exchange:
a song of the retreated ice
for its own absence, rich and strange –
worth nothing, since beyond all price?

Dear Brother

I send you these few lines

I hope they will find you

*

I am well looked after

I am in a cell by myself

*

I have nothing new to inform you

I am come to this

*

I have to inform you

I am tried and the verdict of guilty

*

I am very sorry

I need not make any excuse

*

I hope you will look to yourself

I will say no more

*

I have made it my study

I am to be made immortal

The Sense of Beauty

Hard is our fate, my dear and unknown friend
George is safe in England and in good health

This King belongs to Glasgow, but what he is
I have no right to think, for I am very idle

Yet, in consequence of this great disappointment
He will undoubtedly die in his bed

However, this is a matter of no importance
My pen is no more garrulous than my tongue

I suppose you have heard all the particulars
I would set them in a proper light; but, bless me

I cannot say who commenced firing
You will forgive me I hope when I confess

I think the Cavalry had fired a shot
We had a young, long, raw, lean Scotchman with us

wounded in a most shocking manner
I write with greater ease than I had thought

The Cavalry took a circular course through the moor
You will not meet with so much to hate at Brussels

I proposed forming a square where we were
the Black Hole at Calcutta on an iceberg

They then asked me what rights I wanted
my mind has been at work all over the world

I said annual Parliaments, and election by ballot
with *health* and *hope* we should be content to live

they looked at one another, and said nothing
it is probable you will hear some complaints against me

I am, Sir, your most obedient servant
I should have liked to cross the water with you

Cleanliness

'Thomas Yool, George Carter and postilion do not
wash in the house nor John Hume the Carter.'
  - *Lady Grisell Baillie's Household Book*, 1692–1733

Dozens of times I've cycled past that big house
buried in the trees under Peniel Heugh
and not once thought about these four men
washing the stables off under the stars.

'You must keep yourself very clean', the mistress
wrote in her memorandum to the servants
and so, once every several weeks
they would stand shirtless, somewhere out of sight

and whatever the weather, cast cold buckets
of water from the burn over their shoulders
all sharing one thin sliver of soap
their bodies bright with lather in the moonlight.

Then, having scrubbed the smell of sharn they laboured
in to nothing, they would hand round a faded
clout to dry with, humming 'And werena
my hert licht' as the tiredness took them.

Ways to the Wood

There are more ways to the wood than one
and so many turns around the sun.

A begun turn is half ended.
There's a crack in the world that may never be mended.

Smooth waters run deep.
Walk with me on this road to sleep.

The thing that's done is not to do
and still I write these words for you.

You come a day after the fair.
You are my oxygen, my air.

No one knows where a blessing may light.
You are my nitrogen, my night.

It's good to sleep in a whole skin
but you're the world I'm sleeping in.

Epistle

'Were I to wish myself anything but what I am,
it would be a hedgehog.'
  – Anne Grant of Laggan, *Letters from the
    Mountains* (1807)

And yet, I cannot wholly wish for it.
It would be wrong to wish myself away
into the hedgerows, where I might forget
what I must not: what it has been to be
a woman of our nineteenth century
who through the insufficiency of men
was forced to earn a living by her pen.

My dear, you do not know the solitude
from which these letters come: the distances
of landscapes like Lochaber, which collude
with mountains in us – inner emptiness
with no Fort George, no inward Inverness
to break the wild monotony of thought.
My dear, you do not know how I have fought.

Know I must write to you by candlelight
once my eight living children are abed.
Four others sleep outside. Know that tonight
the rain beats loud enough to wake the dead
upon the slate between my nodding head
and heaven – or the cold infinity
of absence which it sometimes seems to me.

Forgive me this: I am not self-contained
as Friedrich Schlegel the philosopher
whose works have reached us even here, has claimed
the hedgehog is – a beast with spikes for fur
which this intriguing German would compare
to an artistic fragment: marble hacked
to bits; poems where the muse's voice has cracked

mid-sentence, breaking off into the void
like my four children, slipping suddenly
out of existence; as my husband did
and as this letter, unavoidably,
must do when I have nothing left to say
so sign it, leaving something beautiful:
a silence which no speech can ever fill.

The Lichens of Scotland (IV)

Rhendeer Lichen | Brown tipt Rhendeer Lichen
Short white Trident Lichen | Great white Trident Lichen

Branched horned Lichen | Forked Lichen
Prickly distorted Lichen | Little brown prickly Lichen

Black horned Wrack Lichen | Crisped warty alpine Lichen
Round headed Coralline Lichen | Brittle alpine Coralline Lichen

The officinal stringy Lichen | Bearded Lichen
Blackish Mane Lichen | Wiry straggling Lichen

Black hard Wool Lichen | Black Lace Lichen
Little black tufted Lichen | Common rough Lichen,
    without shields

Gold wiry Lichen | Upright flowering Lichen

Handaxe

Whoever was responsible
for this tool, warming in my hand,
it must have taken them an age
to craft, chipping away until
at last the form they meant to find
inside stone started to emerge.

I hold the coldness of it close –
an object heavier perhaps
than I expected it to be –
admiring how the brown veins cross
contours of greyish green, to knap
which would have been like surgery

or sorcery: a spell they cast
to make the winter disappear
that little faster, whiled away
as one blow at a time they eased
a precious thing into the air
and darkness claimed another day.

Under my desk lamp's steady light
I tilt it, trying to picture how
whoever shaped it so would watch
their own hearth draw the gleam from it –
someone whose name I'll never know
though I half-feel our fingers touch.

Broch

For all the fear they once held back
these walls will never speak of it
but as waves break against the rocks
below, I fancy I can hear
stone straining to articulate
a sense of something in the haar.

Squinting into the skeins which fill
the bay, I wonder if a shape
seen for half seconds was a sail
or my imagination, gone
in search of a marauding ship
as eyes before mine might have done.

Then it turns out to be a gull
weaving between two draggled strands
of fog, vanishing in the swirl –
and for the most part this would be
as much as my precursors found
for all their studying the sea.

Poor souls, forever questioning
their intuition as they stared
at the horizon while one long
watch bled without result into
the next, until a dark speck stirred
on the horizon line and grew.

Nectovelius

His real name hides behind its Latin version:
three or four syllables in an unwritten
dialect, echoing faintly in the mirk
of Orcus' gullet.

Twenty-nine when he died, by then he had served
eight winters with the Thracians: a Brigante
who, though his grandfather might have resisted,
fought for the Romans.

Whatever else there was to say about him,
the carver of his tombstone, found near Falkirk
in the eighteen thirties, had no room for more
so left unstated.

A few traces of red paint on the letters
seem to suggest a world of vanished colour –
the green bracken, the yellow gorse, the purple
of the ancient heath.

Or, as the ones who buried him believed
would happen, the bright flicker of his spirit
as it drifted down, shedding definition
amidst the grey shades.

Ricagambeda

Her name survives in one inscription, found
near Ecclefechan where the Romans left it:
five syllables enduring underground
for an unspoken age, until the pit
in which they lay so long – stone-choked, unlit –
was opened and again somebody read
aloud, bringing a god back from the dead.

Ricagambeda, whom the Tungrian
auxiliaries once worshipped, feeding her
on black-woolled sheep, bent coins, perhaps a man
if desperate; whose wishes they'd infer
watching birds' flight patterns, or dry leaves stir
upon the breeze; of whom they were afraid
till with the name the fear too was mislaid.

A god of furrowed earth and twisted trees
or, as it might well be, a god of cloud
heavy with thunder; of the laden bees
busying home, or of the worsted shroud
fate stitches for us: all might be allowed
as fitting functions for a fiction caught
in its undoing, for which I spare this thought.

Then spare another for whoever carved
her only altar, but for which she'd be
nameless as them – a thing forever starved
of even that small sustenance which we
bestow when we invoke a deity
as I do now, filling my lungs with air
to offer this not-quite-lost name a prayer.

Fishing

as summer ends
we let our minds

wander on water
reading the river

like a book
from which we take

whatever sense
we can as silence

shifts between
each line cast on

its troubled surface

Notes on the poems

Ogham | pg. 19
This sequence comprises three acrostic responses to semi-decipherable early medieval Ogham inscriptions from Scotland.

Sleepwalking | pg. 23
This poem comprises found text from *A Collection of Gaelic Proverbs and Familiar Phrases Based on Macintosh's Collection*, ed. Alexander Nicolson (1882), juxtaposed with text from Hannah Arendt, *The Origins of Totalitarianism* (1951).

Highland Vowels | pg. 24
Sources: *A Collection of Gaelic Proverbs and Familiar Phrases Based on Macintosh's Collection*, ed. Alexander Nicolson (Edinburgh: 1882) and, distantly, Rimbaud, 'Voyelles'.

An Unstatistical Account | pg. 28
This poem is composed entirely of found text from the twenty-first volume of the first *Statistical Account of Scotland Drawn Up from the Communications of the Ministers of the Different Parishes* (Edinburgh: William Creech, 1799).

Bone | pg. 42
Source: *Jamieson's Dictionary of the Scottish Language* (Edinburgh, 1885), p. 61.

Breath | pg. 44
Source: *Jamieson's Dictionary of the Scottish Language* (Edinburgh, 1885), p. 73.

Those Unheard | pg. 48

This sequence comprises a series of reverse musical cryptograms from the Skene Mandore MS, with each word corresponding to a specific note in the tune in question.

Dear Brother | pg. 52

Source: the prison correspondence of the radical weaver John Baird in the months prior to his execution at Stirling for the crime of high treason, on 8th September 1820, as published in Peter Berresford Ellis and Seumas Mac a'Ghobainn, *The Radical Rising: The Scottish Insurrection of 1820* (Edinburgh: Birlinn, 1970: 2016).

The Sense of Beauty | pg. 54

This poem combines natural pentameters taken from Keats' letters of 1820 with those occurring in the Scottish radical Andrew Hardie's prison correspondence prior to his execution for high treason the same year.

Ways to the Wood | pg. 57

Source: Allan Ramsay, *The Scottish Proverbs or, The Wise Sayings of the Old People of Scotland* (Stirling: William McNie, 1827).

The Lichens of Scotland (I-IV) | pgs. 18, 34, 45 & 60

Source: The Rev'd John Lightfoot, *Flora Scotica: or, a systematic arrangement, in the Linnaean method, of the native plants of Scotland and the Hebrides*, Vol. II, (London: B. White, 1777).

Acknowledgements

Heartfelt thanks to my family, my parents and siblings especially, as well as all the friends who have, knowingly and unknowingly, helped this book into being.

Thanks also to the Veitch family for all their support.

Thanks to everyone at Moniack Mhor for a truly wonderful three weeks in the Highlands as 2019 Jessie Kesson Fellow – and thanks to Creative Scotland for supporting this.

Thanks to Andrew, Becky and David for hosting me in Cornwall as 2019 Grammarsow poet-in-residence. Thanks also to the Edwin Morgan Trust (EMT) for generously funding my travel to and from Cornwall.

Thanks to Jonathan, Liz and everyone else in the Zellig Group, where some of these poems first found their form.

I'm grateful to the British Council, the EMT, Modern Poetry in Translation, the Scottish Poetry Library and StAnza for the opportunity to participate in projects which saw versions of my poems emerge in Arabic, Friesian and Russian.

My 2016 Robert Louis Stevenson Fellowship in Grez-sur-Loing, France – supported by the Scottish Book Trust and funded by Creative Scotland – was a wonderful waypoint on the road to writing this book.

Thanks to Duncan Lockerbie and everyone else at Tapsalteerie for giving my work a home.

About the Poet

Stewart Sanderson is a poet from Scotland. Three times shortlisted for the Edwin Morgan Poetry Award (2014, 2016, 2020), he has also received an Eric Gregory Award (2015), as well as Robert Louis Stevenson (2016) and Jessie Kesson Fellowships (2019). Widely published in magazines and anthologies, he has performed internationally and participated in translation exchange projects involving writers from Friesland, North Africa and Russia.

A first pamphlet of poems, *Fios,* was published by Tapsalteerie in 2015, and a second, *An Offering,* also published by Tapsalteerie, came out in 2018. *The Sleep Road* is his first full length collection.

www.stewartsandersonpoetry.com
@stewartasanders

Tapsalteerie is an award-winning Scottish poetry publishing house based in rural Aberdeenshire. We produce an eclectic range of publications with a focus on new poets and innovative writing.

www.tapsalteerie.co.uk